EMBRACING LOVE

BY LIZ ADAMSON

THE ULTIMATE GUIDES TO EMOTIONAL FREEDOM

Embracing Love

Published by Diviniti publishing Ltd.
6, Elm Walk, Aylesford, Kent.
Tel: 01622 792866

1st Edition.

Printed in Hong Kong

ISBN 1 901923 44 4

LOVE

Love is the highest expression that we are able to experience. Having said this, it often seems to be a very elusive quality. I will endeavour to reveal the complexities of love in all its different guises and give ways in which we can invite it into our lives as our natural state.

WHAT IS LOVE?

Love defies description. Thousands of poets, songwriters and philosophers have tried to put the experience of love into words and music with varying degrees of success. Love is an abstract feeling and it is almost easier to describe what it is not, than what it is.

Love is a state of **BEING**. We often associate love as being with and for specific people. This is in fact inaccurate. These people are simply the catalysts that have allowed us to connect with this wonderful state of being. Love is exquisite. We may feel it in many different ways. It is the feeling we have when we see a spectacular sunset or a rainbow. It is that moment of connection when we silently share a joke with someone. It is the feeling when we hold a child in our arms and know that it totally trusts us. It is the feeling that we have when we create something beautiful and we are proud of our achievement. We often find that the times when we are experiencing love are just fleeting moments and if we try and cling onto it, the feeling seems to elude us. However, love is our normal state of being and we are meant to feel it twenty four hours a day for no other reason than that we choose to.

Love is a word that is bandied about a great deal and yet there are very few people who actually ever experience it in its purest form. This is because it becomes tinged and diluted by many other emotions which can sometimes totally obscure the underlying feelings of love.

LOVE IS AN ENERGY

Every single thing on this planet is made up of energy. The vibration of that energy will decide what form it takes. Things that are tangible will have a lower vibration. Colour, sound and light will have a much higher vibration.

The highest vibration of energy that there is on Earth is **LOVE**. It transcends all other forms of energy and it is the ultimate height that we can aspire to.

Our purpose on Earth is to evolve. This evolution is created by raising our own personal vibration to a higher and higher level. This is done by releasing fear, which works at a very low dense vibration and to embrace love in a stronger, more intense way. This is a gradual process and everything we need, in order to bring this about will be given to us. This will primarily involve having our fears brought to our attention, so that we can let them go. However, the majority of the population have forgotten the fact that they are here to evolve. When these fears show themselves, we get stuck in them and believe them to be real. This then keeps our energy at a heavy low ebb, which in turn blots out the love vibration. Love energy follows all the laws of physics. It can neither be created nor destroyed, it just changes form. It needs to flow and it comes from a limitless source. Any love energy we bring in and then send out into the world will be immediately replaced.

LOVE AND FEAR

There are only two things on this planet. There is love and there is fear. Absolutely everything we experience is created out of one or other of these feelings. Obviously they appear in many different guises, some of which may be quite difficult to associate with the originator.

We will be familiar with some of the ways in which fear appears. Anger, hurt, guilt, shame, jealousy, control, manipulation, judgement, criticism, loss, scarcity and lack are just a few that we might experience. The way that we can recognise when we are in a fear state is by how we feel. If we do <u>not</u> feel good then we are working with one or more of these negative qualities. For most of us the fear state is the most natural and normal to be in. To such an extent that we may measure a good day as being one where we only experience low grade fear. Right from the word go, we learn fear in our mother's womb.

It is the ego that constantly feeds us our fears and if we believe it, then we manifest it as our reality. However, the fact is that **FEAR IS ALWAYS AN ILLUSION**. This may seem to be a very radical statement, when we see the degree to which it ruins and controls our lives. The whole world is participating in this illusion and consequently perpetuating it to such an extent that we have completely lost sight of what is real. We are **ALL** acting out this illusion. The only thing I can equate it to is the great Santa Claus conspiracy. While children believe in Santa Claus, he is very real for them. They will even take on improbabilities like the fact that he visits every single child in the world in one night or the fact that this big man comes down narrow chimneys and is still clean at the end of it. We might address these issues by saying that he is magic, so he can do anything. However, this particular illusion is nothing compared to the preposterous conspiracy that has created fear. Fear does not exist in reality and yet it is the overriding force that is destroying our world.

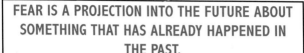

FEAR IS A PROJECTION INTO THE FUTURE ABOUT SOMETHING THAT HAS ALREADY HAPPENED IN THE PAST.

Fear and worry are **ALWAYS** about something that may or may not happen in the future. Even when something fearful is happening, our fear will be about the consequences of it, rather than the reality right now. If and when the thing does happen, we will usually experience one of the by-products of fear like anger and hurt. For many people there may almost be a sense of relief when the fear is realised because then they can **DO** something about it. We are powerless to do something about a thing that has not yet happened and may well not happen. Consequently we may spend a great deal of time and effort, making sure that we do not put ourselves in a position where we could end up realising some of our fears. We then limit our lives to such an extent that we exist only at a very basic level.

It is essential that we begin to burst the bubble of illusion, if we are to survive as a species on this planet. Fear always seeks to destroy before we are destroyed. As a result of this we are doing an excellent job of self destruction in the name of survival. There is only this moment in time and in reality, in this moment we have all we need and want. What we think, feel and believe in this moment is going to create our reality in the next moment. We are so powerful that we create whatever we **CHOOSE** to believe whether it is an illusion or not.

Another analogy I use to describe the illusion of fear is with the mirror. If we stand in front of a mirror, we see a reflection of ourselves. This reflection is not who we are, it is an inverted **IMAGE** of who we are. It does not exist other than as a distorted projection of ourselves. If we then believe this reflection to be who we are and we act accordingly, we lose sight of who we truly are.

FEAR IS AN INVERSION OF LOVE AND IT DOES NOT EXIST IN REALITY.

Every single thought, word or action is either sponsored by love or fear. When we make no conscious choice as to which feeling is going to manifest, then our passive choice will usually be fear. The reason for this is that fear is very assertive. It does not need to be invited into our lives in order to be there. Love on the other hand does. It will only appear in our lives as a result of a conscious decision. The more unconscious and unaware we are, the more fear we will bring into the world and our lives.

Fear creates drama. If we are living a very dramatic existence, then we are allowing fear to write the script. In reality everyone is living the fantasy of a drama of their own creation. We may explore all sorts of feelings and experiences along the way. Ultimately we are here to write the great masterpiece where we choose to experience love in all of its different guises in every moment. We can only do this when we are reminded of the great truth, which is that **WE ARE THE AUTHORS OF OUR LIVES**.

LOVE IS ALL THERE IS

In reality love is all there is. Every experience or expression of ourselves that we have will have love at its core. Even if this is simply there to show us how we are choosing not to acknowledge love. Just as we have polarities of hot and cold, the degree of cold we feel is the amount of hot that is mixed in. It is always there but to a lesser and lesser degree, the further we go down the spectrum. In our spectrum of love and fear, there is always love contained in even the most fearful experiences.

Love wants us to learn and grow and expand and this is done by searching for and finding it in every single moment, no matter what is going on in our external world. There would be no challenge or growth to find love in a Utopian world that hands it to us on a platter. Yet what an achievement it is to find and experience love amongst all the pain, fear and anger that we have created. This is indeed a Herculean task. Yet as more and more people manage to do this, we will begin to turn the tide and make this world into the paradise that it is in reality. We have only to look at the perfection of nature when it has not been tainted by man, to see what is in store for us.

When we can acknowledge that **LOVE** is our natural state and begin to choose it and manifest it in our reality, then we can pave the way for others to do and be the same.

LOVE IS
ALL THERE IS
ANYTHING ELSE
IS AN
ILLUSION

LOVE AND ITS BY-PRODUCTS

LOVE IS THE HIGHEST EXPRESSION OF THE HUMAN EXPERIENCE THAT THERE IS

Love is our summit of Everest, but fortunately it is a great deal more accessible. Love comes in many different forms that we can relate to. Sometimes it is easier to experience love through these qualities because they are more tangible and we can learn how to utilise them in our lives in very practical ways. I will go into details about many of the different guises in which love appears. Many of these will eliminate the negative fear by-products thus making it easier for us to instate **LOVE** as the motivating force behind everything that we think, do and are.

Some of the sidekicks to love are truth, honesty, trust, joy, compassion, beauty, wisdom, abundance, creativity, enlightenment and many more.

LOVE IS THE LIGHT THAT WILL LEAD US OUT OF THE DARKNESS

LOVE AND TRUTH

Truth is the highest expression of love that there is. The truth we are referring to here involves honesty and integrity with ourselves. It means revealing our true authentic selves without fear of judgement or persecution.

When we are true to ourselves, when we express and live our truth in every single moment, when we are happy for others to see us in all our truth, then we have **TRULY** mastered the human condition and we are free. Every single decision and choice is based on what is right for us and is not tainted by the opinions and rules that are being thrust onto us from society, religions and governments.

When we are true to ourselves we are completely open. There is no part of us that is hidden or that we would not want others to see. We walk our talk and live out our truth every day.

When we do this we may well appear to threaten others. It is important that we do not hide ourselves once again in order to make them feel comfortable with themselves.

Every by-product of love has an equal opposite quality in the fear stable. In the case of truth, it is shame. Shame believes that there are parts of us that are unacceptable and therefore need to be covered up and hidden from the world. Much of our existence then becomes about preventing others from seeing us and finding out our shameful secrets. We then create elaborate facades behind which to hide our shame. We make sure that no one gets close enough to find out who we really are. The reality is that anything that we feel shame about is simply an unhealed illusion. Who we **TRULY** are is far more worthy than anyone we could pretend to be. We are perfection, therefore there could not be anything about us that we would want to hide or be ashamed of.

Truth and honesty can be abused when they are

applied to other people. We often camouflage judgement and criticism behind a self-righteous sense of truth. If we do not like the way someone has their hair or the outfit they are wearing, we may tell them so because we think it is the honest thing to do, we are not coming from a position of love. We are causing hurt or anger in the other person and we do not have the right to say how another person behaves.

Often we are so detached from our true selves that our journey to love is to connect, understand and have a relationship with our **TRUE** selves. This relationship is far more fulfilling than any we can create on a human level and will form the blueprint for all the relationships we have with others.

LOVE AND TRUST

Trust is a very important quality that we need to bring on board on the way to experiencing love in our lives. Implicit within trust is the knowledge that everything is taken care of and whatever we need and want is provided for us in the perfect moment. For many people this may seem to be a tall order because their experience of life has shown them a very different picture.

Where there is an absence of trust, there will be a tendency to get caught up in the illusion of scarcity and fear. However we <u>choose</u> to perceive a situation is how it manifests for us. If we only see what is lacking or what we <u>need</u>, we are failing to acknowledge the opportunities and the positive benefits of what we have right now.

Trust is the antidote to fear and worry, which are the most destructive things there are in the world. So we can see that instating trust as part of our natural way is extremely healing. Fear and worry are always about something that may or may not happen in the future. We waste vast amounts of time and energy worrying about things that <u>never</u> happen, causing untold damage to the body and blotting out any joy we may have felt in that time. Trust says that whatever happens in the future is for our highest good and anything that is challenging, we have the resources to deal with.

We often replace trust with hope. It may seem as if hope is a positive word and therefore it would have the same effect. However, when we use the word hope, we are actually saying, "I would like it to turn out well, but it probably won't so I had better prepare myself for the worst." Hope shows up as a negative word when being muscle tested in the body. Every time we find ourselves using the word hope, we can begin to replace it with trust.

Trust is something that we have to learn to bring into our lives. When we do this, we will notice an immediate difference in how we feel and respond to situations that occur. Each time we become aware of fear or worry, we can instate trust in its place and see the illusion of fear dissolve in front of our eyes.

EMBRACING TRUST

1) Be aware that everything that happens is ultimately for your highest good, even when there is a challenge attached.

2) Begin to abolish worry from your life.

3) Every time you find yourself worrying, **STOP**.

4) Immediately **CHOOSE** to bring in trust. Have a statement of trust to hand, for instance;

I TRUST THAT EVERYTHING IS TAKEN CARE OF, AT THE HIGHEST LEVEL.

or **I TRUST THAT ALL MY NEEDS AND WANTS ARE PROVIDED IN THE PERFECT MOMENT.**

5) Keep saying this statement until the feelings of worry or fear subside.

6) Repeat the process each time fear or worry arise.

7) Become aware of how often you use the word hope.

8) Each time it comes to your attention, replace it with trust.

9) Notice how trust not only makes you feel better in the moment but also draws positive miraculous things into your life.

LOVE AND WISDOM

Wisdom is another by-product of love that has been distorted and misunderstood. King Solomon and the legend of Merlin, personify wisdom. Knowledge, learning or intelligence are often mistaken for wisdom. Many people try to attain wisdom through these avenues without success.

We all have access to wisdom but many people have lost the art of connecting with it. This is because we may equate wisdom with the mind and thinking. This is one place that we do not find it. We think if we apply logic and analysis to a problem, then we will find the solution. Sadly, other than in practical situations, this does not work. Any issue or problem that deals with the human condition, does not fit into any logical or mathematical equations.

Wisdom does not come through thoughts but through feelings. We use our intuition to connect with Universal wisdom and the perfect solution or understanding can then be presented to us. In order to get in touch with our wisdom, we have to develop our intuition, which is the means by which it has of communicating with us. Our intuition or gut feeling as some people term it, is naturally in place for every single person. It can sometimes be obscured from us by the negative feelings which reside in the same area of the solar plexus. If we want to increase our intuitive gifts, we have only to disconnect from the mind, which can block and distort the information. We may also need to release and clear emotions like anger, hurt, fear and guilt. As we do this, we get much stronger impressions and feelings about our lives and what we need to understand.

Wisdom will always create a win for everyone involved in a particular issue. It would never see anyone as being bad, wrong or to blame for a situation. However, it gently points out what serves us and what does not. It will also give us the insight as to why other people are behaving in the way they are. This way we can understand them instead of condemning them. There is always a perfect solution to every problem and we will know when we have reached it because it will feel right.

The main thing that wisdom gives us is the ability to **PERCEIVE** everything that happens to us from a positive perspective. This means that whatever we are confronted with in life we will still **FEEL GOOD**.

EMBRACING WISDOM

1) Begin to work with your intuition or gut feelings.

2)   If this connection is weak, then there may be some emotional clearing to be done.

3)   In order to get an answer, you have to first ask the question.

4)   Make sure that the question is clear and that there is a definite yes or no answer.

5)   Breathe into the solar plexus to connect with your intuition.

6)   Do not engage your mind or allow your mind to analyse the information you get.

7)   Once you get an answer, check whether it feels right.

8)   If so, act upon it as soon as possible. Do not get into a debate about it in your mind.

9)   Intuition is like a muscle that needs to be exercised. The more you use it the stronger and more effective it becomes.

10)   **TRUST** the wisdom that you get.

11)   Thank it each time you receive information.

LOVE AND COMPASSION

Compassion is an extremely powerful tool of love. Built into compassion is understanding. When we understand the motives and actions of others, we can react with compassion instead of condemnation.

Compassion is the opposite quality to judgement and criticism. Whenever people judge, criticise or act in any way negatively towards us, it is usually because they are coming from a position of fear, hurt or ignorance. Compassion understands this and instead of reacting to their negative behaviour, it sees the underlying cause of it and gives a positive response.

It is important not to confuse compassion with pity. Pity will disempower people and turn them into victims. Compassion on the other hand will seek to empower them and offer any assistance that may be required or is acceptable.

Empathy is an important aspect of compassion. We understand where that person is coming from and how it feels to be in that position, we react accordingly. When we disconnect from our feelings, we lose the ability to empathise. This can be very dangerous, since we have no concept of how our behaviour affects others. When we empathise, we actually put ourselves in the other person's shoes for a moment and we know how we would want someone to react to us. We are then able to do this. It is important with compassion, that we do not take other peoples' feelings or problems onto ourselves. This simply doubles the problem and solves nothing. Empower the other person to find the answers that they require.

EMBRACING COMPASSION

1)   When faced with the pain or negativity of others, **STOP**, before you react to them equally negatively.

2)   Do not judge or criticise them.

3)   Use your wisdom to understand what is going on behind their behaviour.

4)   Empathise with them and note how you would feel in the same situation.

5)   React in a way that meets others' needs and empowers them, without reinforcing their negativity.

6)   Take note when the best thing to do is nothing at all.

7)   In your mind send that person love and compassion.

EVERYTHING WE DO THINK AND SAY WILL EITHER BE SPONSORED BY LOVE OR FEAR

LOVE AND POWER

Love is the ultimate power. Many songs have been written about the power of love but very few of us have experienced it at its optimal level.

Most of our understanding of power is distorted by the ego and fear. The things that we see as being powerful in our society are the complete opposite of our true power. These include money, status, physical strength, control and manipulation, tyranny and many others. We can always tell the difference between ego power and true power. Ego power will only be created out of disempowering others. It will say, "I have more than you", or "I am better than you", or "If you don't do as I say, I have the power to hurt you", or "if you don't do as I say, I can take something that you value away from you", If we believe these things to be true, then we give our power away to these people or institutions. This then perpetuates the illusion of power.

True power on the other hand, always seeks to empower other people, to elevate them to a higher level. It knows that we are **SO** powerful that we create everything that we think, do and are. With just a thought we can manifest our heart's desire. True power puts love into every facet and equation, so that it cannot be misused or abused in any way. This is important to remember because many people suppress their power since they are frightened of using it in the wrong way. This is just the means by which the ego prevents us from accessing our power. Once again this is an illusion.

It is essential to recognise that no one is able to take power from us. We can only give it away. This will either be a conscious or unconscious decision. Whichever it is, we can always consciously choose to take it back. There is nothing that anyone can take from us or do to us that cannot be replaced or healed. When we **KNOW** this, we have no fear of it happening and when we have this, it won't happen because we are not creating it.

When we access our power, we have a sense of limitlessness and within the knowledge that we can create anything comes the understanding that we only create the things that we need or will enhance our lives in some way. We often will want things when we can't have them. If we can have anything then we are much more choosy.

EMBRACING POWER

1) Begin to be aware of how you see power. Is it ego or true power?

2) How do you use power in your life?

3) Do you often feel powerless?

4) If so, who or what do you give your power to?

5) Do you try and disempower others in order to feel powerful?

6) Begin to empower other people. Make them feel good about themselves. Compliment them and point out their strengths, not weaknesses.

7)   Note that when you give power to others, you must have it already or you would not have it to give.

8)   Empower yourself as you would other people. Give yourself encouragement and praise. Above all be kind to yourself.

9)   Choose to believe in the limitlessness of your power and slowly build on it.

10)   Our sense of power is dependent on what we believe and know. The degree of power we have is created out of our willingness to acknowledge it.

11)   Remember that true power will always benefit mankind as a whole.

WHEN WE DENY LOVE, WE BRING STRUGGLE INTO OUR LIVES

LOVE AND ACCEPTANCE

Acceptance is another important love quality. The fact is that we cannot truly love someone unless we are willing to accept them just as they are.

We often fall in love with a person's potential rather than who they actually are in that moment. We then put a great deal of energy into trying to get them to live up to their potential, so that they can be worthy of our love. When they inevitably do not, we withdraw our love from them, feeling very let down.

Acceptance needs to be exercised in every area of life and when it is, we are completely set free. The first place we can work with acceptance is with ourselves. We can only love ourselves if we totally accept how we look, our abilities and the choices we have made. Once we reach a point of acceptance, we can allow any changes we want to make, to take place. What we resist persists.

Self-acceptance is probably one of the hardest things to achieve because our egos are always telling us our shortcomings or how badly we compare with others. If we believe this negative propaganda, we will never be content with who we are.

The next area of acceptance that we can work with is the acceptance of others. This is most particularly those that we live or work in close proximity with. This includes all their annoying habits, their moods and negative behaviour. This may seem like a very tall order. When we allow ourselves to be annoyed, upset or angry by the words or actions of others, we are handing them our power on a platter. How we feel and what kind of day we have is totally dependent on other people and how they are. Acceptance is the only way that we can take our power back and for us to decide how we feel and if we are going to create a positive day for ourselves. Every time we find ourselves reacting to or being affected by other people, we have allowed ourselves to be hooked. We must then immediately detach the hook and instate acceptance. Anything that someone does will no longer touch us. It is almost as if we have taken a step back and are observing the situation without being a part of it.

The third area of acceptance is with all the things that happen to us or around us. We cannot control the things that happen on a conscious level so we need to accept them. We can also take acceptance to a higher level by deciding that whatever happens is for our highest good and looking for the benefits within the situation. Sometimes this will involve some very creative thinking but once we arrive at a good conclusion or are able to laugh at the situation, the positive energy will come in. Once again we are only able to change a situation once we have accepted it. For instance, if we had planned a picnic and on the day in question it is pouring with rain, we may cancel the arrangements and rage at the heavens for spoiling our plans. We could accept the weather as it is and look for ways to create an equally good day. We could have the picnic under cover or choose to go to the cinema instead. Either way we can decide to have every bit as much fun as we would on a sunny day.

When we are in a total state of acceptance, we are free to be happy, no matter what is happening and what other people are choosing to do and be.

EMBRACING ACCEPTANCE

1)   Look at the different parts of yourself that you find it difficult to accept.

2)   Do you spend a great deal of time focusing on what you perceive to be your bad points?

3)   Catch yourself when you begin to have negative thoughts about yourself and **STOP**.

4)   Repeat the following statement until the negativity subsides.

I LOVE AND ACCEPT MYSELF UNCONDITIONALLY.

5)   Make a conscious decision each day to accept yourself just as you are.

6) Become aware when you are annoyed or upset or adversely affected by people around you.

7) Know that each time you have allowed yourself to be hooked.

8) Mentally unhook yourself from the person and bring in a statement of acceptance.

9) **CHOOSE** to see their behaviour or habits to be endearing or funny, this will remove the negative charge on the situation.

10) Know that everything that happens to us is ultimately for our highest good.

11) When something happens that feels unacceptable, look for the lesson, test or positive aspect of it.

12) Surrender and don't fight it.

For instance if you are caught in a three hour traffic jam, you are powerless to do anything about it so **ACCEPT** it. Then look for something positive to fill that time. Listen to a play on the radio, or work out a new creative project in your head or just relax and rest.

Joy is how we show our love in the world. When we are in a joyful state, we exude positive energy and this can be very contagious.

When we are totally connected to our true loving selves, joy becomes our natural state to be in. We have good will for all and sundry and the negativity of others does not touch us.

For many people, joy is an alien concept, they have never been shown or given the opportunity to express joy in their lives. This will usually be created in childhood where fear, worry and struggle were the norm. Children are naturally joyful creatures and a child that does not play or laugh is exhibiting signs that all is not well at home. If we did not have much joy in childhood, then we will not know how to create it as an adult, even though our circumstances do not prohibit it. This may be a skill that needs to be rediscovered.

The negative qualities that correspond with joy are pain and sadness. These things will obscure any joy we have inside, so that we are no longer aware of its existence. Our pain is an illusion that we have created and that we experience as our reality. We are usually not aware that we are unconsciously **CHOOSING** to feel pain and sadness instead of joy. Joy and happiness is a decision that we make. It is an active choice and not a passive one. We can decide to inject joy into everything we do, no matter how mundane it may be.

We are often looking for things and people to **MAKE** us happy and joyful. This is a very tall order, since nothing can do this and yet **WE** can make anything a happy and joyful experience, simply by connecting with our true loving selves and bringing it into whatever we do.

Laughter and fun are the quickest ways to lighten a situation. It is impossible to feel miserable while we are laughing. It is also very infectious. If someone is laughing, we find that we do too, even when we don't know what is funny. If we take life too seriously, then that is what it will become. **LIFE IS TOO IMPORTANT TO BE TAKEN SERIOUSLY.** If we lighten up and see the funny side of things, even the biggest challenges are easier to cope with.

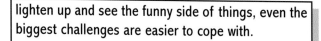

EMBRACING JOY

1)   Remember that joy is our means of spreading love out into the world.

2)   Notice whether you are a naturally joyful person.

3)   Do you look to other people to make you happy?

4)   Do you look for situations or material things to make you happy?

5)   Do you make an effort to give joy to others?

6)   Happiness and joy are a decision.

7)   Begin to choose joy in every moment.

8)   Create a test for yourself by choosing to bring joy into an activity that you do not usually enjoy. This may require some creative thinking. Put some music on, invite a friend over, open a bottle of

wine, be silly while you do it.

9)   Notice if you are unconsciously choosing pain and suffering over joy.

10) If this is a pattern of yours, find the source of the pain and clear it.

11) Stay in the moment.

YOU CAN ONLY EXPERIENCE JOY, WHEN YOU ARE PRESENT IN EACH AND EVERY MOMENT

LOVE IS
ETERNAL
ONCE GIVEN
IT MAY NEVER
BE RETRACTED

LOVE AND FREEDOM

Love will set us free. It has no expectations, no demands, no needs that have to be fulfilled, nothing that we have to do in order to receive or give it. It just **IS**.

When we put love behind every thought, word and action, we are incapable of hurting others or of being hurt. We become one with the highest aspect of ourselves, which does not feel or recognise fear or any of its by-products. **WE ARE TRULY FREE WHEN WE ESCAPE FROM THE SELF MADE TYRANNY OF FEAR**. We need to know that just as it was we who incarcerated ourselves in fear in the first place, we are also the only ones with the key to freedom. **LOVE** is that key.

Love is the light that dispels the darkness. It is the reality that removes the illusions. It is the healer that extinguishes all pain and struggle. It is the miracle worker. There is nothing on this planet that enough love can't cure. There is also nothing negative that a lack of love has not created. We would think therefore that it would be simple to bring in love and live happily ever after. However the vast majority of the population are so caught up in the drama of illusion and are so busy acting it out that they are not aware of the alternative.

The only way to be totally free is to banish the legacy of fear from our lives and instate love as our natural way of being.

Love is free and limitless, it costs nothing, it is effortless to perform. When there is struggle and a lack of energy, it is because we are blocking love from coming into our lives.

EMBRACING FREEDOM

1)   Notice the extent to which you are imprisoned by fear and negativity.

2)   Do you believe that you have the power to free yourself?

3)   Do you think you deserve to be free?

4)   Can you choose to believe that struggle, pain and strife are an illusion that you have bought into?

5)   Begin to acknowledge that whatever you choose to believe becomes your reality.

6)   Allow love to be your reality.

7)   Be aware of the help and guidance that is available to you if you choose love.

8)   **TOTAL FREEDOM IS YOUR REWARD.**

LOVE OF SELF

It is true to say that if we do not love ourselves, we cannot love others. This statement may be met with protestations of denial. Our ego based society frowns on love of self, thinking it smacks of selfishness and vanity. So I will amend the statement and say, we cannot give love to another person if we have not found it in ourselves first.

The source of all love is in our true and highest selves, which is pure love. If we do not access this part within us, then what we perceive to be love is actually something else. It is impossible to give something if we do not have it in the first place.

We <u>all</u> have this unlimited source of love within us and various situations will be the catalyst to reaching this aspect. When we fall "in love" we tap into our true selves. When a mother bonds with her new born baby, she may experience feelings of love that are very intense. Love is just love, it is a state of

BEING. We perceive that we have love for certain people but they are simply the catalysts that help us to reach this part of our **BEING**.

When we love others, we love ourselves, it is impossible not to. However, it is important that we do not become dependent on others in order to experience love. We want to reach a point where we are in a state of love anyway and we simply extend that feeling to those we come in contact with.

We know when we have reached a point of self love. We feel like we are "in love" all the time but this is not aimed at any external person or thing. It is internalised into our true selves. We are then not reliant on the behaviour or presence of other people for our feelings of love. We have them all the time for ourselves simply because we exist. This gives us the freedom to express our love in any way we choose. We do not **HAVE** to be in a relationship because we are having a totally fulfilling relationship with ourselves, and we are in control of how that relationship unfolds. The power is in our own hands and we have not given it away to another person who may abuse it.

When we are in a state of love for ourselves, we then want to share this wonderful state with others. We do not **NEED** anything from them because we are able to provide it for ourselves. We come into the relationship unencumbered by the baggage of demands, expectations, needs and fear of rejection or abandonment. This frees the relationship up to work at the highest level of expression and experience of love.

Love of self, far from being greedy or selfish is the first step in our transforming ourselves and the world. We cannot teach what we have not learned. We can all spout the theory but it is putting it into practice that counts. Love's natural impulse is to flow and it comes from an unlimited source, so the more we give out, the more we get back. The challenge then becomes how to maximise our output. This is unconditional so we do not expect anything back from the people we give it to, only from the **SOURCE**.

EMBRACING LOVE OF SELF

1)   Be aware that love comes from inside you and not from external sources.

2)   Begin to have a relationship with yourself. Treat yourself as you would want to be treated by others. Give yourself praise and compliments.

3)   Connect with things and people that make you feel good.

4)   Take some time every day to **BE** with yourself without having to do anything.

5)   Learn to connect with your inner self through your breath.

6)   Use your intuition to communicate with your inner self. When you do this, you will get a sense of the degree of love there is for you.

7)   You will know when you have made the connection because you **FEEL** good.

8)   Make the connection for as long as possible and as often as you can until this becomes your natural state of **BEING**.

UNCONDITIONAL LOVE

In a way we should not need to label love as being unconditional, since this is implicit within the quality. Sadly we are always putting conditions on our love and are prone to withdraw it if those conditions are not met.

IF LOVE IS CONDITIONAL,
IT IS NOT LOVE.

There are many things that masquerade as love in our lives. These include infatuation, lust, attraction, need, dependency and obsession. When we are in any of these modes, we will usually use the word love to describe our feelings. Love is probably the most misused word in the Universe. Love once given is eternal, it cannot be retracted. We cannot fall out of love, just as it is inaccurate to say that we fall "in" love. We are either in a state of love or we have allowed it to be obscured by the illusions of fear, hurt, jealousy and resentment.

If we say we love someone and then hurt them or put them down or in any way disrespect them, **IT IS NOT LOVE**. Love is incapable of such actions. If we want to punish or control other people, **IT IS NOT LOVE**. If we judge, nag or criticise and don't listen to what those close to us have to say, **IT IS NOT LOVE**. If we love someone on the condition that they love us back or if they behave or look in a certain way, **IT IS NOT LOVE**.

Love just is, it does not depend on any external criteria. It is sad to say that the only totally unconditional love that many people experience is with their pets. This is often because that is what the pet gives us, unconditional love and devotion. They do not care what we look like, they forgive us no matter how we treat them and they are always there for us. It is perhaps an even sadder observation that there are many people who are so damaged and disconnected from their true selves that they do not experience

ANY form of genuine love in their lives. I would hate to speculate how many people come into this category.

Unconditional love or real love can only come into our lives if we have already connected with it in ourselves first. When we give unconditionally, we are more inclined to get it back from others. Even if we don't, it doesn't matter because it is unconditional. We also don't **NEED** it because we have already created it for ourselves. This puts the power firmly in our own hands. We are not rendered powerless by putting the source of our love into another person's hands who may not be relied on to come up with the goods.

EMBRACING UNCONDITIONAL LOVE

1)   Be aware of the things in your life that may be masquerading as love. For instance, need, attraction etc.

2)   Do you want or expect people to be a certain way in order to get your love?

3)   Are you aware of others putting conditions and expectations on you?

4)   Can you tap into and connect with the source of real love in you?

5)   Extend this love to those around you.

6)   Whenever you become aware that your love is conditional, then you have disconnected again.

7)   Make the necessary changes to reconnect.

8)   If this is hard then there may be some damage from the past that is obscuring it. Release this and then reconnect.

LOVE

IS THE

KEY TO

EVERYTHING

LOVE AND NEED

Need is the thing that most often masquerades as love. Most relationships are based on an exchange of needs. The unspoken deal is that we will attempt to meet our partner's needs while they are doing the same for us. If we perceive that they are not doing this, then we will stop doing what they need and want. Needs are what create a relationship, our inability to meet those needs is almost always what will end the relationship. Along with this will come a great deal of hurt, anger and resentment.

Needs are created out of what we **PERCEIVE** that we did not receive in childhood. We then put the full weight of expectation on our partner to give us what we have not got. However, when we believe that we don't have it, no matter how much our partner attempts to give it to us, it does not change our underlying sense of lack. As the relationship progresses, the tendency is to give less and less, which reinforces our needs. A relationship that is created on this basis will not work long term. It creates a great deal of disillusion and we then move on to another partner, hoping that they will fulfil our needs.

It is only when we reach the understanding that we do not **NEED** anything, everything we need and want comes to us in the perfect moment and that we do not have to depend on another person to give it to us. This obviously takes a huge leap of faith but whatever we choose to **PERCEIVE** becomes our reality. When we take need out of a relationship, we open the way to experience true love at the deepest core level.

The other side of the need equation is dependency. When someone who is dependent matches up with someone who needs to be needed, this will appear to be a match made in heaven. However, this is very deceptive since there is very little room for growth here. If one member of the partnership dies or decides to move on, it can be catastrophic for the other one.

It is essential that we heal and change our understanding about our needs, so that we get our needs met easily, without expecting others to meet them. When we give to others the things that we think we need, then we become aware that we already have it or we would not have it to give. This can dispel the illusion of our neediness.

RELEASING NEEDS FROM OUR LIVES

1)   Become aware of the needs you have that you expect other people to fill.
2)   How many of these can be met by your giving them to yourself?
3)   Did you have these things consistently in childhood?
4)   How can you change your perception of childhood to see that you had them all the time?
5)   What needs have you put onto your partner or partners?

6)   Have they been able to meet them?

7)   How do you react if and when they do not do so?

8)   What needs have been put onto you by your partners?

9)   How did you feel about having these demands put onto you?

10) Have you had relationships that broke up because you or they did not get their needs met?

11) See how you can elevate your partnership to a higher level where need does not play a part.

WE CAN ONLY TRULY LOVE WHEN THERE IS NOTHING THAT WE NEED

LOVE AND RELATIONSHIPS

The one area of life where we expect to give and receive love is in one to one relationships. We get into them in order to be loved and in the short term we may feel loved but the cracks will soon appear. We can see by the amount of relationships breaking up that something is very wrong in the way we conduct our partnerships.

From the point when we first separate from our true selves, we are looking to replace the love that we had received from that quarter. This separation takes place when we first experience fear which then obscures the reality of who we are. This will usually occur very early on in our development, often even in the womb. We first of all look to our parents to give us the love we are missing. They may not be capable of giving the amount or depth of love we want. From pubity onwards we begin to separate from our parents and we then look to relationships to make us feel loved. Added to the expectation of being loved, we put onto our partner all the things that we needed and did not receive in childhood. We look to them to make everything right for us. This is of course an impossible task and the relationship will founder at the point where we realise we are not getting our needs met.

So where does love come into relationships? When we first meet someone and we go through the phases of attraction and infatuation, we access, even if only fleetingly, our true selves and we **FEEL** love. We **THINK** that this love is for and about the person that we are attracted to. Some lucky people manage to remain open and connected to this place for a few months or on and off for a few years. At the point where the ego and fear, hurt, resentment or jealousy comes into the relationship, we disconnect from our loving true selves and we no longer perceive ourselves to be "in love" with our partner and we no longer feel loved. At this point, need and dependency will have taken over from the love. If there are children or joint finances involved this will

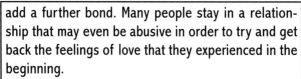
add a further bond. Many people stay in a relationship that may even be abusive in order to try and get back the feelings of love that they experienced in the beginning.

We need to grasp the fact that this love we are constantly looking for outside ourselves is actually contained within us all along. The good news in all of this is that we have complete power and control over our love and we are not dependent on being in love or loved. We have no fear about our partner rejecting or abandoning us because they are not the source of our love, **WE ARE**. This understanding will free us up totally.

Once we have grasped this, we might ask why we need relationships. We are here to expand our love and to extend it as widely as possible. When two people come together who have both accessed the love within them, the whole is greater than the sum of all the parts. A relationship is about intimacy. Intimacy means sharing ourselves at the deepest core level. When we achieve this, the feelings of love we have intensify. We are able to experience higher vibrations. This is immensely powerful. Sadly there are few people who have actually managed to achieve this consistently. However, it is the ultimate goal within a relationship that we can work towards.

One of the main reasons that so many people do not manage to maintain intimacy past the early stages of the relationship, is the illusion of hurt and pain. We may have been hurt in previous relationships or by our parents in childhood. In which case we may not be willing to open up and allow intimacy, for fear of being hurt. We may also give our partner the benefit of the doubt until he or she does something to hurt us, then we shut down and deny them access to our inner selves. For instance, our partner may not phone or cancel a date or forget our birthday, we choose to feel hurt by these actions and in order not to feel hurt again, we shut them out. However, this will almost always create the very scenario that it was designed to prevent, because we end up being hurt anyway. Hurt is an illusion and we have it because we **CHOOSE** to perceive a situation to be an attack on us. We can go into the very same situation with a perspective of acceptance, tolerance or patience and there is not hurt.

Most of our damage from childhood will emerge in a relationship and it is really important to be aware of what we are projecting onto our partner that actually has nothing to do with them whatsoever. If we have had a very difficult or traumatic childhood, it will be harder to have a successful relationship. The reason for this is that most of our feelings and emotions are contained in the child aspect of ourselves and this is the part that often engages within the relationship. If we had a childhood full of fun, laughter and creativity, then we will bring these qualities to the relationship and it will be enriched as a result. The damaged child will bring a very different legacy to the union, filled with fear, hurt, anger and mistrust. Most of us are a very good mixture of the damaged and joyful child and we will alternate between the two.

A successful relationship takes a great deal of understanding and work. If we can make sure that no matter what challenges come up in the partnership, the love is always the predominant feeling and motivating force within it.

Remember, **LOVE CONQUERS ALL.**

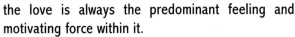

BRINGING LOVE INTO RELATIONSHIPS

1)   Can you pin point times in your life when you have felt love or "in love" with another person. This is in its pure unadulterated state, where it is not tinged with fear, hurt or disillusion?

2)   This is your natural state and it can be accessed by you at any time, regardless of whether you are in a relationship or not.

3)   Within your relationships what are the things that end up obscuring the love?

4)   To what extent are your relationships based on need and dependency?

5)   Do you feel love for your partner when he or she appears to meet your needs?

6)   What needs do you expect your partner to meet? To be loved, respected, taken care of, etc.

7) Can you begin to perceive that you already have the things you need and you are the only one that can procure them anyway?

8) Do you choose to take on hurt in the relationship?

9) Do you then withdraw from your partner?

10) Do you try and hurt your partner back when you feel hurt?

11) Bring in acceptance for what ever your partner says, does or is. This does not mean being a doormat and taking abuse. If this is the case you need to consider why you are in the relationship.

12) Is there damage from childhood creeping into the relationship and trying to destroy it?

13) If so remove it from the arena of the relationship and do the necessary work to clear and release it.

14) When you connect with your **TRUE** self, you have everything you need and want.

THE RELATIONSHIP CAN THEN BE ABOUT WHAT YOU CAN GIVE AND NOT WHAT YOU RECEIVE.

LOVE, JEALOUSY AND POSSESSIVENESS

Many people confuse jealousy and possessiveness with love. We may feel that if someone is jealous if we look at another man or woman, then this is proof that they love us. Some people even go out of their way to make their partner jealous in order to feel loved.

Jealousy and love are in fact very far removed from each other. When we are jealous, **IT IS NOT LOVE**. Jealousy is usually created in childhood. The most common cause of jealousy is the arrival of a sibling that seems to take our mother's love and attentions away from us. This creates a pattern that will in adulthood replay again and again. Our fear is that our partner will see someone they like better than us. Our self-esteem is usually pretty low, so we also believe that there are thousands of people better than us that they would rather be with. We are consequently always looking for signs that they have found one of them. We often create a self fulfilling prophecy here as our jealousy will often drive our partner away. This will then reinforce the whole process. Jealousy is an extremely destructive quality and it will effectively block out any love we have.

Possessiveness is another thing that may seem to masquerade as love in our lives. When we take on someone and treat them as a possession, we do not love them. The source of possessiveness is also in childhood. When we openly give love and perceive it to be rejected or not returned when we are small, we will often have an issue with possessiveness in relationships as an adult. With both possessiveness and jealousy there will be an element of control. If we can control our partner and the environment we are in, then everything will be all right. There may be abuse that occurs in the relationship as a result. In extreme cases the person may not even be allowed out of the house or to talk to anyone unless their partner is there to monitor the situation. Once again this will effectively kill any love that is present in the union and create a climate of extreme negativity. The possessive partner will almost always give the reason for their behaviour as being that they love them. The other half will usually be desperate for love and may even believe this to be true. This will be the thing that keeps them in this destructive situation.

Love knows that we do not own anything or anyone in reality. Love will always want to create a climate of openness, honesty and freedom. Love accepts that we have no right to control another person. Love also recognises that we have the right to love more than one person.

RELEASING JEALOUSY AND POSSESSIVENESS

1)   Is jealousy or possessiveness a problem for you?

2)   Is it always there or does it only arise at various points in the relationship?

3)   Do you make this problem your partner's responsibility? For instance, do you tell them that as long as they do not talk to or look at a member of the opposite sex, then your jealousy will not arise.

4)   Does your partner have an issue with jealousy?

5)   If so, do you allow him or her to control your behaviour?

6)   Do you see jealousy as a demonstration of love?

7)   Do you test the love by making your partner jealous?

8)   If jealousy is present in your relationship, **IT IS NOT LOVE** and it will end up destroying the positive aspects of it.

9)   Find the source of the jealousy in childhood and release the feelings and beliefs that created it.

10)   Know that if you grant someone their freedom, they will come back to you willingly. If you imprison them, they will want to escape.

LOVE AND ABUNDANCE

Abundance is another quality of love. We often associate the word with money but it actually has a much broader application.

Abundance is having more than enough for all our needs, wants and desires. This covers things like love, joy, wisdom, fun, creativity and money. All these things come from an unlimited source and consequently, it will never be diminished or run out, no matter how much we use. When we have this understanding, we only use as much as we need at any time. There is no reason to stock pile or save for a rainy day because it will **ALWAYS** be available to us. This probably seems too good to be true but it is the reality that is accessible to every single one of us.

The opposite qualities of abundance are scarcity and lack. This is the principle that the vast majority of the population live by and they end up creating that reality. Scarcity puts out that there is not enough or that there is a limited source and some people will get more than their fair share, while others will get less. This then sets up a two tier system of the haves and have nots. Those that do not have, resent those that do and some will even go a step further to try and relieve them of their money, through theft or deception. Those that have, are terrified of becoming a have not and may consequently seek to get a bigger slice of the pie than they actually need or want. Many of the problems in the world are created out of the illusion of scarcity and lack. Strangely enough, many poorer societies have a greater grasp of abundance than the richer western nations.

Abundance has nothing to do with how much we have. It is the state of **BEING**. When we are in this state of being, we know that we have everything that we need or want, even if in material terms, we have very little. Our lack of abundance often causes us to buy or hold onto things that we neither need nor want. We hope that we will feel abundant by our ability to get these things. Many people get themselves into a great deal of debt in order to feel better about themselves, only to feel worse in the end. When we feel empty inside, it is due to the fact that we have separated from our true loving selves. We then look to find things to fill the empty space inside. Some people use drugs, alcohol or food to do this, others may attempt to fill themselves with money, cars or things. Ultimately none of these things will give us more than a momentary buzz. The **ONLY** way to fill the emptiness inside is to reconnect with who we are. When we do this, we are in a state of **LOVE** and **ABUNDANCE**, and we have no need to look to external or material things to fulfil us because we are already **FULFILLED**.

There is an irony in the state of abundance, which is that at the point where we **PERCEIVE** that we do not need anything, **EVERYTHING** becomes available to us. We then only choose to bring things into our lives that will either make them easier or are beautiful and enhance the quality of our lives. Everything else is surplus to requirements and will waste our energy, either by cluttering up our lives or by needing a great deal of maintenance or time spent on them. This is where greed and abundance are so diverse. With abundance, we can have it all, so we only want what we need and desire. With greed, there is only a limited amount so we want it all.

Abundance frees us up to devote all our energies to what is important and expansive. We do not spend most of our time trying to survive by doing work that is just there to keep body and soul together. When we are in this mode, we are disconnected from the unlimited source of energy and abundance. Consequently, we are tired and drained and we have nothing left to channel into the real work that we are here to do.

It is impossible not to be abundant when we are in a state of real love. They come as part of the same package and they allow us to experience ourselves and our lives at the highest level.

EMBRACING ABUNDANCE

1) To what extent do you buy into scarcity consciousness?

2) Do you perceive your resources to be limited?

3) Do you struggle to survive on a material level?

4) Are there things you want that you can't afford?

5) Do you do work that you don't enjoy simply for the money?

6) Can you remember times in your life when you had more than enough for all your needs, wants and desires?

7) If so, how did this **FEEL**?

8) Do you look to money or material things to fulfil you?

9) Does this work?

10) When feelings of lack come in, bring yourself back to this moment and ask yourself; "In this second are all my needs taken care of?" In reality

the answer to this question is always yes. This knowledge can bring in a state of abundance.

11)   Look at how nature works, and how totally abundant it is. We are part of nature and if we are being natural, then our abundance is guaranteed.

12)   Choose to believe that **ALL** your needs, wants and desires are taken care of and then see what turns up. This will be what you **DO** in fact need. If you allow your ego to determine your needs, you will be stuck in scarcity and lack.

WE ACHIEVE MASTERY WHEN WE CHOOSE LOVE IN EVERY THOUGHT, WORD AND ACTION

THERE IS

NOTHING

THAT ENOUGH

LOVE

CANNOT HEAL

LOVE AND SOCIETY

Our society is governed by ego principles and it has very set ideas about love and what is and is not acceptable. The fact is that if it is <u>real</u> love, there is nothing that can be wrong or taboo in its expression.

Our society says that we are meant to find the **ONE** person in the world that we can love for the rest of our lives and once we have done this we are not allowed to love anybody else. It also says that we cannot love more than one person at the same time.

Society says that we can love our children but we must treat them in a certain way. We must suppress their anger and hurt. We must use fear and the threat of violence to control their behaviour. We subject them to abuse. We make them feel ashamed and inhibited about their bodies. We make them think that they have to look a certain way or own certain things in order to be acceptable. We help them to disconnect from their true selves, so that they need drugs, alcohol, cigarettes or sex in order to try and fill the emptiness inside. All this is done in the name of love!

Society also has created very warped views around sex. In its essence sex is a wonderful expression of love. What it has become is a multi million pound industry of exploitation. It is about money, power and control. It has become a leisure activity rather than a loving one. Children are under huge pressure to have sex at an earlier and earlier age, when they are not emotionally equipped to handle it. Love and sex are not synonymous. In fact the gulf between them is growing larger and larger.

Society does not feel comfortable with demonstrations of real love. We become embarrassed or ashamed for showing or saying how we love another person. It does not approve of love between two people of the same sex. This is deemed to be unnatural. The only thing that **IS** unnatural is the suppression and denial of love, which is our only natural state to be in.

UNDERSTANDING LOVE

LOVE IS ETERNAL – Love once accessed and given, cannot be retracted. It lasts forever and will transcend everything, even death.

LOVE IS A CHOICE – Love is available to us at all times, we either choose to access and feel it or we don't. If we are passively waiting for love to come to us, we may be in for a long wait.

DENIAL OF LOVE – When we deny love in our lives, we are creating struggle for ourselves. If we are in a state of struggle, we may need to look at how we block love from coming to us.

LOVE AND ENLIGHTENMENT – Love is what will lighten up our lives. Love is also the light that dispels the darkness. It shows fear to be the illusion that it is.

LOVE AND FEAR – In every single moment our thoughts, words and actions are either being sponsored by love or fear. One creates joy, miracles and bliss, the other creates pain, struggle and powerlessness. The decision is ours.

LOVE AND HURT – If love hurts then it is not love. Love is incapable of being in or causing pain. If we perceive that love hurts, we either have to change our perception or see that times when this has occurred was not about love but need, infatuation or obsession.

LOVE IS TRANSPARENT – When we love there is nothing to hide. We are completely open.

LOVE IS IN THE PRESENT — Love is a state of being and in order to experience it , we have to be in THIS moment or we miss it. If we are constantly projecting into the future, we bring in fear and worry. If we are harking back to the past, we experience, hurt, anger and regret. This moment is filled with love.

LOVE AND THE OUTER WORLD — If we are looking to find love in our outer world without accessing it first in our inner one, we will always be disappointed.

WHAT WOULD LOVE DO? — Whenever there is a decision or choice to be made, it is simplified by this one question. What would love do?

I wish that you may embrace love in your life.

Liz Adamson is available for one to one sessions, talks and workshops.
Contact: Flat 3, Hamptons, Hadlow, Tonbridge, Kent, TN11 9SR.
E-mail. liz@edenbook.co.uk

Available by Liz Adamson.

The Ultimate Guides To Emotions.
Releasing Anger   £4.95
Releasing Hurt and Sadness   £4.95
Embracing Love   £4.95
Embracing Happiness   £4.95

The Ultimate Guide to Relationships
                                     £7.95
The Ultimate Guide to Abundance and Prosperity   £7.95

Contact: Diviniti Publishing Ltd.
6, Elm Walk, Aylesford, Kent ME20 7LS
Tel: 01622 792866.
E-Mail hypnosis@diviniti.co.uk